WILL YOU JOIN
THE CAUSE OF GLOBAL MISSIONS?

DAVID ALAN BLACK

Energion Publications
Gonzalez, Florida

2012

Cover Design: Jason Neufeld (jasonneufelddesign.com)

ISBN10: 1-893729-18-4
ISBN13: 978-1-893729-18-6

Energion Publications
P. O. Box 841
Gonzalez, FL 32560

850-525-3916
www.energionpubs.com

To the memory of my translator James
— brother, fellow worker, fellow soldier (Phil. 2:25) —
who gave his all in the cause of the Gospel.
His name should not be forgotten.

TABLE OF CONTENTS

Foreword.. vii
Will You Join the Cause of Global Missions?........................... 1
1. Missions is the calling of every follower of Jesus.................2
2. Missions is at your doorstep......................................5
3. Missions is a global, cooperative movement.......................8
4. Missions requires a counter-cultural lifestyle...................10
James... 12
Conclusion... 14
An Invitation..19
Global Missions Commitment...20

FOREWORD

Christianity at its core has little to do with buildings, programs, or events. At its heart we find the MESSAGE of God — the unchanging, supernatural Gospel — which compels those changed by it to give their lives to the MISSION of God — the fulfillment of the Great Commission.

My friend Dave Black gets this. Don't let the fact that he is a highly regarded Greek scholar, accomplished author, and winsome professor hide the reality that above all else he is a missionary. He and his bride Becky have been faithful missionaries to their neighbors and to the nations, including annual trips to Ethiopia.

Dave lives as a missionary because he is convinced that every follower of Christ above all else, regardless of vocation or location, has the high honor of serving Christ as a missionary. In these pages you will glean from his wisdom and feel his heart. We live in a time where the Western church is seeing a much needed, growing revolution shifting from professional preachers to living witnesses who live the mission. We need less superstars and more servants, and this book explains why.

If you follow Christ there is within you a fire, a passion for your life to matter for Him. It was Zinzendorf who said, "Preach the gospel, and die forgotten." May God raise a generation with that passion, and may we see the nations reached to the glory of God and for the sake of the Gospel.

Alvin L. Reid, PhD
Professor of Evangelism & Student Ministry
Bailey Smith Chair of Evangelism
Southeastern Baptist Theological Seminary

WILL YOU JOIN THE CAUSE OF GLOBAL MISSIONS?

We must be global Christians with a global vision because our God is a global God.
— John Stott

God is at work all around the world today, completing His task of global evangelization. And He wants to use all of us in that process. He is releasing the potential of His church into global missions as never before.

Would you like to become part of the Big Story of what God is doing worldwide? Would you like to be on mission for Him? You will have to begin by putting first things first. There need to be powerful motives if we are to pluck up the courage to start this daunting task. As a matter of fact, there are at least four of them.

1. Missions is the calling of every follower of Jesus.

Don't think for a moment that it is more honorable to go to seminary and become a pastor than it is to serve God faithfully as a nurse or salesperson. Missions is the intended vocation for the whole people of God, no matter what your occupation may be. The apostle Paul never viewed his secular tentmaking job as a hindrance to his ministry. Quite the contrary. He viewed his job in the workaday world as indispensable to his church planting strategy. The distorted and unbiblical division between "sacred" and "secular" has gone on long enough. It is time to get rid of it — once and for all. God is inviting *all* of us to participate with *all* that we have in our lives. You don't need a degree in missions to do this. All you need is a surrendered heart. Why squander your life doing anything else?

Luther, Calvin, and the Anabaptists agreed that there is only one "divine vocation" for all Christians who accept their role as the people of God, and that is to minister for Christ in our various spheres of life. My wife Becky is a fulltime housewife and I am a fulltime Greek professor, but those are our jobs. Our business is the *Gospel business* — fulltime, 24/7/365. In the New Testament, we find no fixed forms, organizational structures, or ranking of "fulltime professionals" in the church. Ministry belongs to the whole people of God. Christians are to be Christ's servants in *all sectors of life*. Under the direct leadership of the Head, the whole Body penetrates the whole world (including our own neighborhoods) with the Good News. We are Jesus' disciples, followers, learners, witnesses, workers, and, if need be, martyrs. Christ ascended for the specific purpose of "preparing God's people for works of service" (Eph. 4:12). It is unmistakably clear that the term "priest" as used in the New Testament does not refer to officiates in a church building but describes all Christians in every nation of the world in their role as fulltime Christian ministers.

For several years now I've been studying the missionary

movement in North America and beyond. I believe we are on the verge of an era when insourcing missions will become *the* strategy for achieving global evangelization. A strategy that depends on outsourcing the work to paid professionals is not going to get the job done. Outsourcing will be around for a while longer because it is what everyone is used to. But insourcing will require a wholly different mindset. It's not just about producing more missionaries. It's about creating a completely different kind of environment — a collaborative environment in which everyday people like you and me are constantly thinking about how to generate towel and basin ministries both at home and around the globe.

When you start insourcing for more effective mission work, all kinds of good things begin to happen. For Becky and me, this has meant a deeper working relationship with Christians all over the world. It has meant getting to work side by side with local churches in countries such as Ethiopia, where resources and manpower are most needed. It has meant streamlining efficiency as top-heavy bureaucracies are bypassed. It has meant more sustainable relationships between churches in the U.S. and churches in other nations. Moreover, the more you are seen as insourcing, the more people will want to get involved as they begin to realize that they too can play a part in global missions.

This is the dynamic that I, as a seminary professor, am tracking most closely. What strikes me the most about the new generation of seminary students is how *ordinary* they are. They are just everyday Christians who care deeply about the Great Commission and are willing to forego the American Dream in order to accomplish it. Moreover, they are beginning to realize that the church's greatest asset is the so-called laity, people at the grass roots who think missionally and globally. There are so many trends, so many hopeful signs, that I dare not predict how it will all play out. But getting this right is going to be critical for the church of the twenty-first century. The work is so difficult, and the stakes are so high, that we can't afford to sit on the fence any longer.

I will take it a step further and say that the greatest thing any local church could do for itself, for its people, and for the world is to publicly state its intention to place the Great Commission first in everything it does. The church's reason for being is utterly tied up with the process of getting Christians to live and act as salt and light in the world, as our Lord commanded. The church must be equipped to serve in the world precisely because it is not of this world. It is an upside-down kingdom that moves forward on its knees, casts down evil strongholds through sacrificial love, and opens closed doors. As never before, we need God's servants who are willing to risk life and limb to preach the uncompromising Word of God. Excuses won't do. None of us is too young or too old to learn the power of voluntary service for others in the name of Jesus. And when we have learned to embrace this attitude of self-denial, we will begin to experience the abundant life described by Jesus in John 10:10.

2. Missions is at your doorstep.

"Global" missions means just that — the mission field is anywhere in the world, including right where you live. The unnamed believers who took the Gospel to Antioch (Acts 11) were simply living out their Christianity in the midst of their daily existence. What better way to be a witness? What better way to be salt and light than to become enmeshed in the fabric of society by working alongside your neighbors and friends? We need to learn to view our employees, our co-workers, our fellow students as our mission field. What's more, God has brought the world to our doorstep. By reaching out to the immigrants and international students in our midst with the love of Christ, we can make a significant contribution to fulfilling the Great Commission. More than one third of all students who study abroad are enrolled at U.S. institutions. Many of them experience a high degree of alienation and loneliness. Everyday kindnesses — locating housing or employment for them — can open doors for the Gospel. Develop the habit of embracing every international whom God brings into your sphere of influence.

Again, we can't leave the work to the so-called professionals. One of the major lessons taught in the New Testament is the biblical centrality of the local church. Each and every congregation is to be an evangelistic, witnessing community to its surrounding neighbors. "The Lord's message rang out from you," wrote Paul to the Thessalonians (1 Thess. 1:8), implying that when a church receives the Good News of salvation it has an obligation to pass it on. Our God is a missionary God, and our Lord Jesus Christ commands us to be His witnesses in the entire world, beginning with our own "Jerusalem" (Acts 1:8). This idea that a local church is to be a witnessing community may come as a surprise to some people. When they think of evangelism they think only of professional evangelists and large, city-wide crusades. And this is partly true. God has blessed the work of fulltime evangelists and their

5

efforts to reach whole cities for Christ. The weakness of this approach is that it sometimes leads local congregations to abdicate their own personal responsibility to reach their communities for Christ.

I often hear people complain that witnessing does not come "naturally" for them. With this I agree. Evangelism is not a natural task at all; it is a completely supernatural enterprise. In fact, personal evangelism is utterly impossible unless the Spirit of the Lord Jesus is given free rein in our lives. Thus, while it is our duty to share our faith with others through word and deed, even more it is a divinely-enabled privilege. And unless we learn to view evangelism in those terms — as a great privilege and not merely as a duty to be performed legalistically — we will never be successful in motivating either ourselves or others to share Jesus, no matter how much training we may have had in this or that evangelistic technique or method.

For many of us, the problem is one of inactivity. We genuinely long for our neighbors and friends to come to Christ and be changed forever. But we do nothing about it. And behind it all is a lack of motivation or even a lack of faith that God can use us. We must pray that the same missionary Spirit of the Book of Acts would fall upon us afresh. At the same time, we must beware of counterfeit "fads" in evangelism that ignore the incarnational aspect of missions. How easy it is to reduce witnessing to passing out a tract or placing a bumper sticker on our car, not that those things are bad in and of themselves. We stay aloof from human sin and tragedy. We love the lost, but not sacrificially. It costs us little to leave a tract with our restaurant server. It is far more difficult to engage him or her in conversation. However, the very shape of Christian mission is cross-like. People are receptive to the Gospel when we enter into their suffering.

Many Christians say they are committed to living sacrificially for the sake of the Gospel. But are they? It is a matter of priorities. Biblical evangelism is always costly. And

6

it always combines words with works. Jesus was never content with mere teaching. His was a ministry in which words and works achieved a perfect and beautiful balance. Service was indissolubly linked with preaching. The problem we experience, whenever we think about evangelism, concerns the tension between proclamation and presence. The ideal combination is rarely achieved today, as it was in Jesus' ministry. As John Poulton has said (*A Today Sort of Evangelism*, p. 60), "Christians need to look like what they are talking about." We cannot communicate the Gospel in words only. Evangelism must also include loving deeds. And it must begin at our own doorsteps.

3. Missions is a global, cooperative movement.

Just one generation ago missions was largely the work of large organizations that established "mission stations" in foreign countries. Today, missions is more a partnership between local churches in America with local churches in other nations. We need to repent of our independent, "let's do it our way" mentality. The goal is to build inter-church discipling relationships that last. Unfortunately, many U.S. mission teams fail to coordinate their endeavors with the churches of host locations. Recently a student of mine mentioned that his local church was going to plant a new church in China. I asked him, "Have you ever considered simply going to China and asking the existing churches there how you can come alongside them and help?" Failing to understand and connect with God's already-at-work global purpose is one of the greatest mistakes we can make as churches. More and more local churches in America are forging effective partnerships with local churches in foreign nations, asking how they can best serve the needs in those countries. When done well, everybody benefits through this kind of beautiful partnership, and Christ is honored as His people submit to one another in love. Much of this work is being done, moreover, apart from top-heavy bureaucracies as more and more U.S. churches realize that, according to the New Testament, the local church is the authoritative sending body of the New Testament missionary (see Acts 13).

If churches in America were truly committed to the Great Commission, it would show in a lifestyle that matches our response to a lost and dying world. In Paul's lengthy passage on Christian stewardship (2 Cor. 8-9) he describes the economics of the kingdom. He reminds us of the grace of our Lord Jesus Christ, who became poor for us even though He was rich. Paul adds, "I don't mean that others should have relief while you have hardship. But there should be equity. Your abundance should supply their needs." Can you imagine what would happen if our churches in the U.S. were to grasp this principle of equity and of sharing our wealth and applying it to the needs of the Gospel around the world? Could it be that our materialism is keeping the world in darkness about the Good News? Shocking statistics published recently report that:

> According to the World Christian Encyclopedia of all the money designated for "missions" in the U.S. only 5.4% is used for foreign missions. Of that 5.4%, only 0.37% is used to take the gospel to unreached people who don't have access to the gospel. That's about two cents out of every dollar given to missions! The rest goes towards efforts to further evangelize reached people. (See http://lightthewindow.org/1040_window.html.)

Again, let me stress that there is no one-size-fits-all pattern of giving. All churches are called upon to find ways to prioritize the kingdom as the Holy Spirit directs. The most important principle to keep in mind is to employ material things for the kingdom of God rather than for ourselves. This is the true test of where our priorities lie. God may ask us to forgo building that new sanctuary, give up our Sunday School quarterlies (and use the Bible instead), or sacrifice our padded pews. Many will think you're crazy if you do things like this. The Christian media often measure success in terms of big numbers, big buildings, and big programs. God, I think, measures success differently. He is calling each of us to be a bondslave to a world in need. We are called to be foot-washers for Jesus. We are invited to accept the call to live a life of radical Christian servanthood wherever we are and wherever we go in the world. Today I believe God is calling out an army of Americans who will feel His heartbeat and answer that call.

4. Missions requires a counter-cultural lifestyle.

The American Dream says, "Earn and spend it on yourself." Christ says, "Live to give — to others." We must learn how to live purposefully and to give strategically. Are you placing eternal value on temporal things? Are you caught up in materialism? (Every American is to a degree.) You can learn to become more content with what you have in order to give more of your income to the needs of others as well as to advance the Great Commission. I'm not talking about writing an occasional check for missions. God is looking for people who wake up in the morning focused on allowing the compass of His heart to direct their resources each and every day. We need to think of ourselves as slaves of Christ, totally at the disposal of our Master. As His slaves we will do His will and promote His cause. His lordship over our finances will be absolute.

You see, in the kingdom of God what matters is obedience. The essence of the Christian faith lies in our willingness to walk in the way of Jesus. Paul writes, "The kingdom of God is not in word but in power" (1 Cor. 4:20). In other words, the essence of the kingdom is not theology (word) but practice (deed). We must let go of everything else in this world. We must live as citizens of the kingdom, a kingdom that requires a loyalty surpassing our loyalty to our parents, spouse, church, country, and even our lives. "The kingdom of heaven," said Jesus, "is like a merchant looking for beautiful pearls who, when he had found one pearl of great price, went and sold all that he had and bought it" (Matt. 13:44-46). Kingdom Christians have found the pearl of great price. Like Jesus, they refuse to separate doctrine from practice, word from power. They reject the Constantinian Hybrid that combines the kingdoms of this world with the kingdom of God. What matters to kingdom Christians is what the Scriptures say, not what any man says. If you're serious about being a kingdom Christian, I encourage you to read the teachings of Jesus for yourself. You will quickly discover that the kingdom of God is not an easy road. Jesus' kingdom, unlike earthy kingdoms, is always at war. And King Jesus requires *absolute* loyalty from His citizens.

James

I want you to meet James. James was my translator when I trekked among the Guji tribe in southern Ethiopia a few years ago. He was a young and optimistic 24-year old, freshly graduated from the university. All who knew him loved him. His smile was infectious and so was his passion for the Gospel.

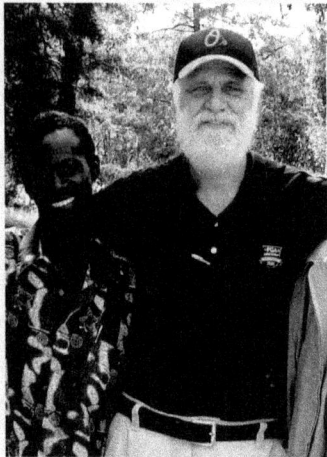

When one of my friends and I decided to minister among the Gujis, we needed a translator who could speak excellent English as well as excellent Orominya (with a passable Guji accent). He would also need courage, in bucketsful. You see, the Gujis hate the Burjis. Not all the Gujis do, but certainly a good number of them do. For centuries they have killed Burjis, often without any apparent cause. In fact, the last two evangelists to work among the Gujis were both murdered. So, the question of the hour was: Who would translate for us? James stood up and volunteered. We told him, "Are you aware of the dangers?" "Yes," he replied, "but the Lord Jesus has told me to go and be your translator." And so for seven days we trekked from Guji village to Guji village, living among the people, eating their food, sharing their life, and telling them of a Savior who loved them so much He sacrificed His best for their sake. After a week the fighting got so bad that the Burji church elders ordered us to return to Burji, and thus our expedition among the Gujis came to an end.

A few weeks after we returned to the States, James wrote me an email. It was short and to the point. "They're looking for me," was all he said. He meant that his enemies were hunting him down to kill him. He had fled to a larger city to

try and lose himself in its anonymity. He failed. A week later we received the news that James had been suffocated in his sleep. He was the first martyr of our work in Ethiopia.

If you were to judge James by normal "American" standards of success, you would have to conclude that he was crazy or at least an absolute idiot. But kingdom people think differently. In the kingdom, "normal" just doesn't cut it any longer. What matters is that we're imitating Jesus and serving others sacrificially. That's what James did. And that's what Epaphroditus did. (Read Phil. 2:25-30.) Paul writes, "He risked his life and nearly died for the sake of the work of Christ, in order to give me the help that you yourselves could not give" (Phil. 2:30). By these standards — living for Christ and helping others — both Epaphroditus and James were winners. Unless a deep, practical, loving care is shown, unless we are willing to give our lives for the sake of others, the mere proclaiming of Good News will be useless.

I'm proud and humbled to have known James. Though he would have detested the moniker, he is a modern-day Epaphroditus. Thank you, James! We love you, we miss you, and we will see you in glory!

Conclusion

The conclusion is inescapable: In light of the commands of our risen Lord and Savior and in view of the present desperate condition of a lost world, we must give everything above our basic necessities to finish the task of world evangelization. We cannot serve God and Wealth at the same time. Money will either be our master or our slave. We are to lay up for ourselves treasure in heaven — not on the earth. 1 John 3:16-18 gives us our marching orders:

> *This is how we can know the love of God, because He laid down His life for us. We too should lay down our lives for our brothers and sisters. Whoever has this world's goods and sees his fellow believer in need and shuts up his compassion for them — how can the love of God dwell in that person? My dear children, we must love not in word or in tongue, but in deed and in truth.*

The whole purpose of the church can be summed up in that one concept: sharing. We are never commanded in the New Testament to do many of the things we are currently doing (paying out lavish salaries, building huge worship centers, etc.). Those things are not evil in and of themselves, of course. But the Bible clearly commands us to "share what we have with God's people who are in need" (Rom. 12:13). What a rebuke this verse is to the pleasure-loving and disobedience of so many Christians and churches today in America! How much longer will we allow our desire for comfort and "the good life" to be the bottleneck that prevents world evangelization?

I'm sure most of you have heard about the discussion going on these days about the relationship of right thinking (orthodoxy) to right living (orthopraxy). In this book I've argued that one can have correct doctrine and yet not be living the Christian life in any meaningful sense. I am convinced that there is absolutely nothing — nothing! — that proves the genuineness of our beliefs as our love for one another and our willingness to lay aside our own agendas in service to the world for which Christ died. I truly believe that we are only promoting cheap grace when we focus on correct doctrine — or, rather, those aspects of doctrine that appeal to us (e.g., Calvinism, Arminianism, Baptist theology, etc.) — instead of allowing belief and action to kiss as we take up the basin and towel in the name of Jesus. Sacrificial living for the sake of others is not a virtue just for those with a special gift of philanthropy. It is at the very core of Christianity.

For the life of me, I can't figure out why we must insist on pitting doctrine against love. There is absolutely nothing more important than love. No other agenda can even begin to compete with it. Nowhere is this more evident than in 1 Pet. 4:8, where Peter writes, "Above all, love each other deeply, because love covers a multitude of sins." Here Peter says that love is "above all," and he insists that we are to have "constant love" for one another. I can't understand why this is so hard to see. Rather than pitting doctrine against love, it is more accurate to say that love is the most foundational doctrine of all. The central place of love in Christianity is clearly seen throughout the New Testament, from the teaching of Jesus (Matt. 22:34-40), to the teaching of Paul (Rom. 12:9-21; 1 Cor. 13:1-7), to the teaching of John (John 13:34-35; 1 John 2:7-11). James, our Lord's brother, puts it this way: "Religion that God our Father accepts as pure and faultless is this: to care for orphans and widows in their distress, and to keep oneself from being polluted by the world" (James 1:27). Again, it is religion *in action* that counts. In fact, I would argue that love in action is the only real solution to the problem of doctrinal division today. True Christian unity is not found in uniformity engineered by men or in external unification, but in Jesus Christ. The worst "solution" to sectarianism is to start yet another theological movement. Yet isn't this precisely what we do? Unable to get along with Paul, Cephas, or Apollos, we start our "Christ-party." "Our doctrine is purer than yours," we insist.

Now let me be clear about what I am not saying here. I am not saying that theology is unimportant. I am not saying that we cannot hold to our own doctrinal distinctives in the Body of Christ. But to do so without love is nothing but noise, writes Paul (1 Cor. 13:1-3). So what should we do? I think a good place to start it to acknowledge that we are not saved by orthodoxy. This is not to say that orthodoxy does not matter. The New Testament abounds in warnings against false teaching and in exhortation to sound doctrine. But if, as I have argued, love is the most important criterion of true orthodoxy, then failure to love must be recognized for what it is — false teaching of the worst kind.

Our Lord was careful again and again to stress the cost of complete devotion to Him. Every prospective follower of Jesus Christ ought to understand that discipleship will cost everything. Belief is only the beginning. Suffering for Christ is the privileged path we are all called upon to follow (Phil. 1:29). In an age when information is substituted for action, this message needs to be understood loud and clear. Jesus insisted that there is no fruit unless the seed first dies. As never before, the church today needs God's servants who are willing not only to believe the uncompromising Word of God but also to give their all to the ultimate mission of the church — world evangelization in our generation. Instead of dividing around our pet doctrines and personalities, we can start praying for and working with everyone who is united with us in the essentials. As Peter says, we have to stoke the fires of love until Christ is on display in our midst. As followers of Jesus, we are meant to enjoy deep fellowship with one another. Under God's great grace, we are called to be *one* with one another. What can create this kind of community? Community cannot be preached. It can only be practiced, and the place to start is with oneself.

I am convinced that the apathy we see in our churches is due not to bad people but to bad theology. I can't help but wonder which came first: the impulse to over-theologize the New Testament, thus removing our personal responsibility to obey the implications of Jesus' teachings, or the tendency to separate thinking from living, doctrine from practice, orthodoxy from orthopraxy. Either way, the answer to bad theology is not no theology but good theology. Let me emphasize again: I love theology! I am all for engaging our minds to their fullest when it comes to the Scriptures. A man who has authored or edited such books as *Interpreting the New Testament*, *Rethinking the Synoptic Problem*, and *Learn to Read New Testament Greek* might well feel justified in calling himself a serious student of the Bible. But the sad reality is that one can write books about the New Testament and yet fail to incarnate the teachings of Jesus in one's own values, beliefs, and practices. And that is precisely my point in this book. *The holiest and most necessary expression of Christian theology is also the most ordinary.* God's grace is experienced in every sphere of life, including such mundane acts as working, eating, and socializing.

This has serious implications for the church. Jesus' disciples enjoyed community simply because Jesus and not a set of dogmas was at the center of their life. They never tried to "build community." They didn't have to. Community was the result of being united in the Christian mission; community emerged naturally when they committed themselves to something bigger than themselves. And so it is in the church today. It is my personal observation that most Christians begin to enjoy genuine community only when they begin to serve the poor, evangelize the lost, and plant churches. The glue that unites them is the missional task of loving their neighbors. A shared sense of mission drives them to community. Their congregations are mission-shaped. Like Jesus, they literally go. For them the Bible, not tradition, is normative, and they hold themselves accountable to each other in love even while they work closely with the surrounding neighborhood, developing strong links between Christians and not-yet Christians.

This incarnational approach to missions is the clear pattern of the New Testament. The church proves its love for God by its love for others. Perhaps as never before in the history of the church, the work of global evangelization will depend on the birth of such missional churches worldwide, churches that understand the importance of the doctrine of lavish love. I commend you to find the methods and forms for doing the same in your local church context.

An Invitation

I would like to conclude this brief study of missions with an "alter" (not altar) call. There is a new movement abroad in the world, and I would like to invite you to be a part of it. It is an incredible revolution, and I am convinced that once you experience what it is all about, you will never be satisfied with anything less.

Christian friend, will you, this very moment, answer Christ's call to take the Gospel to the lost all around you, relationally and relentlessly? General Booth, founder of the Salvation Army, was stung into activity by the words of an atheist who said, "If I believed what you Christians believed, I would crawl across England on my hands and knees, if need be, to tell men about it." Evangelism is not the task of the ordained clergy. All of us are called upon to share the Good News with others. It is simply one beggar telling another beggar where they may find food.

Many Christians have never led anyone to Christ — ever! They don't think that God can use them in this way. I'm here to tell you that God delights in using run-of-the-mill people like you and me to reach others with His love. Once we put ourselves unreservedly at His disposal, and ask Him to use us in His service, He will do so. But we need to ask Him, and to ask earnestly. There is no prayer that He loves to answer more.

It is absolutely essential that we settle this matter, once and for all. It is not enough to love the Lord. It is not enough even to love the Lord and love each other. We must love the Lord, love His people, and love His world, too. Once you have been gripped by the lostness of those who do not know your Lord Jesus Christ, you will need no further incentive to share the Good News with every asset at your disposal.

So...

Will you join the cause of global missions?

GLOBAL MISSIONS COMMITMENT

By God's grace and for His glory alone, I hereby commit my entire life to obeying Christ's Great Commission by becoming a global Christian. Having committed myself to the cause of global missions, I will:

1. Go anywhere God sends me.

2. Give sacrificially of my time, treasure, and talents to live out the call I have heard from Christ.

3. Pray earnestly every day for God's work of global evangelization.

4. Consistently share my faith with non-believers as God opens doors for me.

5. Seek to be Christ to those who don't yet know Him by developing webs of friendship.

6. Seek to mobilize others to become Great Commission Christians.

Signature_____ Date _____.

www.ingramcontent.com/pod-product-compliance
Lightning Source LLC
Chambersburg PA
CBHW060549030426
42337CB00021B/4502